The Donahue Sisters

A Play in One Act

Geraldine Aron

A SAMUEL FRENCH ACTING EDITION

SAMUELFRENCH.COM
SAMUELFRENCH-LONDON.CO.UK

Copyright © 1991 by Geraldine Aron
All Rights Reserved

THE DONAHUE SISTERS is fully protected under the copyright laws of the United States of America, the British Commonwealth, including Canada, and all other countries of the Copyright Union. All rights, including professional and amateur stage productions, recitation, lecturing, public reading, motion picture, radio broadcasting, television and the rights of translation into foreign languages are strictly reserved.

ISBN 978-0-573-13234-6

www.SamuelFrench.com
www.SamuelFrench-London.co.uk

For Production Enquiries

United States and Canada
Info@SamuelFrench.com
1-866-598-8449

United Kingdom and Europe
Theatre@SamuelFrench-London.co.uk
020-7255-4302

Each title is subject to availability from Samuel French, depending upon country of performance. Please be aware that THE DONAHUE SISTERS may not be licensed by Samuel French in your territory. Professional and amateur producers should contact the nearest Samuel French office or licensing partner to verify availability.

CAUTION: Professional and amateur producers are hereby warned that THE DONAHUE SISTERS is subject to a licensing fee. Publication of this play(s) does not imply availability for performance. Both amateurs and professionals considering a production are strongly advised to apply to Samuel French before starting rehearsals, advertising, or booking a theatre. A licensing fee must be paid whether the title(s) is presented for charity or gain and whether or not admission is charged. The professional rights in this play are controlled by the author who may be contacted via Samuel French.

No one shall make any changes in this title(s) for the purpose of production. No part of this book may be reproduced, stored in a retrieval system, or transmitted in any form, by any means, now known or yet to be invented, including mechanical, electronic, photocopying, recording, videotaping, or otherwise, without the prior written permission of the publisher. No one shall upload this title(s), or part of this title(s), to any social media websites.

Minor revisions to the text of this play were made when it was reprinted in 1994, 2006 and again in 2009.

For all enquiries regarding motion picture, television, and other media rights, please contact Samuel French.

The attic of the family home in Ireland, once the sisters' playroom, is the setting for this sinister play. United because of their father's illness, the three women talk of their lives long into the night, until the time comes for the ritual re-enactment of a violent and disturbing incident from their childhood. Departing from the hitherto naturalistic style of the play, the author imaginatively uses the sisters themselves, speaking and acting in unison, to create the persona of the fourth character, the young boy, Dominic. When the ritual is complete things once more return to normal — only now the women would appear to have found an answer to their problems, with the uneasy prospect of the past repeating itself ... Inventive and mysterious, this play is a challenge to both actors and director.

THE DONAHUE SISTERS

This play was first staged by the Druid Theatre Company in 1990 with Ingrid Craigie, Marion O'Dwyer and Katherine O'Toole. The production was directed by Garry Hynes.

This edition is dedicated to my good friend
Sholto Williams

CHARACTERS

Dunya
Rosie
Annie

The action of the play takes place in an attic

Time: the present

Other plays by Geraldine Aron
published by Samuel French

Bar and Ger
A Galway Girl
Joggers
Olive and Hilary
Same Old Moon
The Stanley Parkers
My Brilliant Divorce

THE DONAHUE SISTERS

The attic room, once the playroom of the family home in Ireland, late on a winter night

There is a child-sized table, preferably with a drawer, set with a tray of tea things, beneath which is a Ludo board. The dice and shaker are either in the drawer or hidden behind the table leg. There are also four little chairs decorated with nursery motif transfers and some old-fashioned toys including a doll's cradle containing a soft bodied doll with a large porcelain head. An effective doll's head can be fashioned out of a clay flower pot encased in fabric and concealed with a wig of curly hair. The flower pot can be replaced when it becomes too fragmented. The set would ideally have a trapdoor UR, *with enough under-stage space to allow the actors to appear to enter and exit*

As the CURTAIN *rises the stage is in darkness. An Irish children's choir can be heard singing*

As the Lights come up we discover the three sisters sitting at the table. They face DS, *smiling and perfectly still as if posing for a photograph. Dunya is* L, *aged forty, a sophisticated and expensively dressed New Yorker. Annie is* C, *aged thirty-eight, homely and frumpy. Rosie is* R, *aged forty-two, a Londoner, a little worn out and shabby*

As the choir music fades, church bells can be heard in the distance striking the half-hour. This activates the three women and Rosie pours the tea, while Annie, using tongs, plops a lump of sugar into Dunya's cup

Annie Oh, I forgot, you don't like sugar in yours, do you, Denise?
Dunya No, and I don't answer to the name Denise either.
Annie (*fishing the sugar out with her fingers*) Oh, pardonny-moi! I forgot. So what are you calling yourself these days?
Rosie Dunya. D-u-n-i-a.
Dunya Y.
Annie Why what?
Dunya Dunya with a Y. *Dune*-yah.
Annie Russian again. But 'tis better than Annush*ka*!

Pause

Rosie So. The Donahue sisters meet again. Cheers!

Rosie raises her cup, Annie raises hers, but not Dunya

Annie }
Rosie } (*together*) Cheers.
Dunya I knew he wouldn't die. This trip's a complete waste of time and money—just like the last one. That old bastard will outlive the lot of us.
Rosie Wouldn't you pity him though? All those tubes - and the machines clanking and hissing and bleeping day and night. Just the flick of a switch away from eternal peace, God love him.
Annie Did you notice who the nurse was in Dad's ward?
Dunya (*in a sing-song voice*) Mrs O'Malley.
Annie Remember years ago, when she lost her son. The whole town turned out for the funeral. You'd think they were royalty and the father a chimney sweep.
Rosie The mother seems completely recovered.
Annie Why wouldn't she and he such a bold boy.
Dunya A bold boy. Now there's an expression I haven't heard in a long time.

The three exchange looks

Annie Anyway, the mother's a grand nurse. They say she keeps 'em alive by willpower—doesn't want her ward to get a bad name. So Dad's in the best possible hands.

Dunya (*sarcastically*) God bless him.

Rosie Well, I'm glad it got us together. We must be the world's worst correspondents. If it weren't for Mam we'd never get news of each other. It's unnatural for sisters.

Annie Have ye still got your samplers, girls?

Dunya Our *what*?

Annie Well, thanks very much, the two of you. They took me weeks to embroider. You were supposed to frame them.

Rosie Wait a minute, you mean that linen thing, with the motto stitched on it —

Annie "Divided by land and water, united by family blood. All for one and one for all, the Donahue Sisters stick together".

All three clap their hands twice. For the third clap, Dunya and Rosie clap Annie's upheld hands, briefly creating a linked chain

(*huffily*) So you couldn't be bothered framing them.

Rosie To tell you the truth, I thought mine was a tray cloth, Annie. I had a lot of pleasure out of it though, lovely colours.

Annie (*to Dunya*) And what did you do with yours—use it as a floorcloth?

Dunya I gave it to the kids. They used it as a bedspread for their Barbie dolls.

Annie Great.

Rosie So girls. How's married life?

Dunya Terrific. How's yours?

Rosie Bliss to begin with ... gets better all the time.

Dunya Mr Wonderful.

Annie You met him down St Mary's Hall, didn't you, Rosie? At one of those Saturday night bop sessions. Jesus, they were great.

Rosie I'd fancied him for ages. But he was doing a line with that little fat girl who used to wear white high heels and no stockings in the middle of winter.

Annie Big purple legs on her. A little fat one, but all the fellas were mad about her. What was her name?
Dunya Josie. "She was only a milkman's daughter, but she knew how to pull a pint".
Rosie Fancy you remembering that. Anyway, "a little bird" dropped Alan a line explaining the finer points of Josie's character —

Dunya makes wing-like movements with her arms

—and that was the end of Josie!

All three chuckle

Dunya Were you involved with him that time you thought you were pregnant?
Rosie I beg your pardon?
Annie (*very indignantly*) I never heard that. Why did I never hear about that?
Rosie Because it's a figment of Denise's — I beg your pardon — *Dune-ya*'s imagination.
Dunya If you weren't pregnant, how come you wrote asking me to send you money for an abortion?
Rosie I have no idea what you're talking about. Are you sure this isn't something you invented for one of your novels?
Annie With all due respects, Dunya. I'm sure I'd have known if my own sister was expecting. Sure we slept in the same bed after you went off to America.

Dunya shrugs, bored with the subject

Anyway, let's not be delving into the past. So Alan's still the man of your dreams, is he, Rosie?
Rosie One in a million. What about your Tony? Still crazy about squash?
Annie Bowls these days. He's a league player now. Brilliant at sports, always was. And how's your ould fella, your Guy?

The Donahue Sisters

Dunya Gey. G-u-y, Guy. It's French.
Annie (*rolling her eyes*) Well, how is he, whatever his name is?
Dunya Hunky dory.
Rosie Kids?
Dunya Two.
Rosie (*patiently*) We know you've got two children, Dunya. I was enquiring about their health.
Dunya Hunky dory.
Annie They must be what — twelve and fourteen now. Farah and Pasha. Are they bright?
Dunya They practically glow in the dark.

Pause

Annie Well. Any other news?

Pause

Rosie You both look in great shape, I must say. Do you work out?

Dunya rolls her head languidly

Dunya Every God-damned day.
Annie I work out three times a week. With a double helping of thighs.
Rosie Those thigh exercises are a bit obscene, don't you think? Whenever my Alan catches me doing them, I'm in for a little ole roll in the hay — even in broad daylight, if you please!
Annie Roll in the hay, indeed. Tony and I don't bother our heads with all that stuff. He says it drains a person's energy.
Dunya Is there anything to drink in the house?
Annie Well, Mam might have something left over from Christmas. I'll go down and look.

Annie exits

Rosie She's aged a lot, don't you think?

Dunya We've all aged.
Rosie Yes, but Annie's let herself go. I could hardly keep the shock off my face when she met me at the airport. She's aged ten years in the last five. And fat.
Dunya In the States we prefer to say heavy.
Rosie Is that so? Heavy instead of fat? As in Jack Sprat could eat no heavy... and —
Dunya For God's sake, Rosie, get a grip on yourself.

Annie enters with a large bottle of vodka and three glasses. The bottle appears first, and is placed on the floor near the trapdoor (if this is available)

Annie Vodka, but no tonic. So I don't know what we'll use for mixers.
Rosie There's a lemon in the fridge and I think I spotted a tin of tomatoes down there.

Annie takes her seat. She has no intention of going downstairs again

I'll go.

Rosie exits

Annie Did you notice her hands, Dunya? Sure those are real dishwasher's hands. They must be struggling. Those hands have never had the benefit of a dishwashing machine.
Dunya No dishwasher in this day and age? Dear God.
Annie Well, Tony and I have one, of course. I bet Rosie's living hand to mouth, the poor lamb.
Dunya Serves her right for having four kids.

Rosie enters with a jug of tinned tomatoes and half a lemon

Rosie Here we are!

The Donahue Sisters

Annie pours modest drinks, using the cap of the bottle as a tot measure. Dunya retrieves the bottle and tops up her glass. Annie and Rosie spoon some mashed-up tomato into their drinks. Dunya, holding her glass aloft, adds a single drop of lemon. The others are disapproving and Dunya gives them a challenging look

The three raise their glasses for a toast

The church bell begins to strike the quarter hour

Annie (*tensely*) Is it time?
Dunya Uh-uh. That's the quarter hour.
Rosie
Dunya } (*together*) Cheers.
Annie
Dunya (*picking up her handbag*) Anyone feel like a toke?
Rosie
Annie } (*together*) Sorry?
Dunya A toke, a joint, a spot of weed, a touch of Mary Jane.

Pause

Annie Drugs, is it?

Dunya laughs, rummages in her handbag and withdraws a cigar cylinder. She opens it and produces an extremely large joint

Sweet baby Jesus! You didn't come through Customs with that in your handbag!
Rosie Mick Jagger went to prison for that. It nearly wrecked his career.

Dunya lights a joint, draws deeply and offers it to Annie

Annie You must be joking. Tony would murder me.

Dunya shrugs and offers it to Rosie

Rosie (*pretending sophistication*) No, thanks. A drink's stimulating enough for me.

They watch Dunya carefully, so she puts on a show. She rolls her eyes in her head, lets her jaw drop and throws in a few body jerks. Just as suddenly, she reverts to normal and smiles at her astonished sisters

Annie Have you ever taken crack?
Dunya Of course not. A little cocaine now and then, but not crack. Crack's addictive. (*She offers the joint to Rosie again*)
Rosie Do you just draw on it, like a ciggie?

Dunya demonstrates and offers it again. Rosie takes it cautiously, draws, waits — hands it back

Nothing. I feel exactly the same.

Dunya smiles and offers the joint to Annie

Annie You sure Mammy won't come up?
Dunya Positive. She's gone for the night. I gave her one of my sleeping pills.

Annie takes a series of drags, watched by the others

Annie I feel dizzy from holding my breath, but that's about all.

Pause

Rosie suddenly bursts out laughing. Dunya smiles

What's so funny?
Rosie (*becoming serious with great effort*) I was just thinking about your sampler. When it got too shabby to use as a tray cloth, I used it as a potholder!

The Donahue Sisters

They are all overly amused by this. They try to stop laughing, but soon burst into fresh gales

Dunya I used mine to mop up Pasha's sick one day. It was the only thing to hand. It never recovered.

They all find this hilarious

Annie Tony burnt your novel. He said he didn't want filth lying around the house.

They roar with laughter

Rosie We gave our copy to, to… (*She collapses*)
Dunya A library? A collector?
Rosie (*barely able to speak*) A jumble sale!
Dunya (*not so amused*) With sixty thousand copies in circulation, sweethearts, I guess one or two won't be missed.

The joint goes around again

Rosie crosses her legs and suddenly swings her foot up in the air so that her shoe flies off. She catches it deftly and is delighted with herself

Annie (*with great importance*) About eight years ago, after a meal that included curried lentils, Tony spent the evening passing wind and he hasn't stopped since.

They laugh

Rosie (*suddenly realizing what's been said*) Jesus, that's terrible, Annie. I couldn't live with a man who did that.
Dunya They all end up farting. Guy farts in bed. He says lying down stimulates his colon.
Rosie (*pouring herself a large drink*) I wish you wouldn't use the word fart. It's very low-class. Anyway, that's nonsense. It's

all a question of self-discipline. If they didn't pass wind when they were courting us, why should they pass wind now?
Dunya Because now we're just little old wifeys.

They reflect sadly on this

Rosie half-heartedly tries her shoe trick, but fails to catch it

Rosie Every morning of his life, Alan pulls on his pants. Does up the zip. Fastens the catch. Buckles his belt. And then puts on his shirt.

Pause

Annie What about it?
Rosie To tuck in his shirt, he has to undo everything again. So he makes the same moves twice, every morning of his life.
Annie (*indignantly*) Sure that's the goings-on of an ejit!
Dunya Guy's a very efficient dresser. He has to be. He's having an affair. Screwing a black model.
Rosie I hate that expression, screwing. There's no romance in it.
Annie (*faintly*) Black hearted, do you mean. Or actually black?
Dunya Black as burnt toast. Very tall, very slim. A Grace Jones clone.
Rosie Grace Jones with the bald head?
Annie No, Sinead O'Connor was the baldy. Grace Jones was the one with the *square* head. Anyway, go on, Dunya.
Dunya He's been seeing her for six months. I think this one's serious.
Annie Ah, you poor thing. Does he know you know?
Dunya Sure. He says she's essential to his creative process. I just pay the bills. He's building a mountain of hubcaps this year. It gets harder and harder to be original in New York. He's America's first post Nine Eleven hubbist. (*She laughs despairingly*)

The joint goes round

The Donahue Sisters

Annie I don't know what to say. I really don't. I thought you were as happily married as I am.

Pause

Rosie She probably is.
Annie Meaning?
Rosie (*to Dunya*) Tony never speaks to her. Mam says loads of people have noticed it. Never says a word to her.
Annie There's nothing wrong with a quiet man. Better than a fella who'd be yak yak yakking all day, getting on your nerves. He's grand in every other way.
Dunya Apart from his wind problem. Maybe he's pioneering an entirely new method of communication. Talking through his ass. He'd be a sensation in the States.
Rosie New York's made you very vulgar, Dunya. There was never vulgarity in our family.
Dunya Seriously. How long's this been going on?
Rosie Two years, Mam thinks.
Annie Three years, know-all. Give us another puff on that thing.

The joint goes around

Rosie Alan and I are scared stiff of our kids. They've been terrorizing us since Liam — that's our youngest — was about twelve. If we don't give them money, they lock us in the bathroom. It's awkward, being on the fifth floor. Sometimes we have to get the neighbours to let us out.
Dunya (*to Annie*) Are you telling me he hasn't spoken to you for three years?
Rosie (*glumly*) They beat us up whenever they feel like it.
Annie (*to Dunya*) He clammed up just after his fortieth. Blamed me for killing all the fish in his aquarium. Awful looking things, with their big goggly eyes following me round all day. If we'd had kids like everybody else, he wouldn't have been so obsessed with those *slitherers*.
Rosie (*completely ignored*) Whenever they feel like it—just beat us up.

Annie He accused me of switching off their heater on purpose. We had a tiff over it and he's never spoken to me since. He made a vow. I'm not allowed to speak to him either.
Rosie They took my jewellery ages ago. I've nothing left except my wedding ring — and they only left me that because they couldn't get it off. They've sold most of the household to buy drums and electric guitars. They've formed a group called Car Park Sex. Heavy metal. Even the major appliances. All gone.
Dunya So how does it work? How do you greet each other when he comes home, for example?
Rosie Pearls. Earrings. Watch. All gone.
Annie Well, I smile at him and he gives me a nod.
Rosie As I said, nothing of value left except my wedding ring. (*She holds up her hand, showing the ring*)
Dunya How about "what's for dinner"? How does he handle that?
Annie He uses a process of elimination. (*She swiftly mimes a cow with horns, a chicken flapping its wings and pecking, and a wild-eyed fish, gasping in extremis*)

The other two stare at her

Beef. Chicken. Fish. I just nod when he hits the right one.

Rosie has taken an interest in Annie's mimes

Rosie What's this, then? (*She mimes a chicken as Annie did*)
Dunya Chicken ...

Rosie continues, mimes placing a crown on her head and waves regally

Annie Chicken à la King!
Dunya Now me! (*She mimes a cow*)
Rosie Beef ...

Charade-style, Dunya pulls on the lobe of her ear and points to the others

Rosie (*confused*) Sounds like ...

Annie Sounds like "you". Beef stew! You see how easy it is? But don't you be putting my private life into one of your smutty novels.

Dunya Nobody would believe it. They'd say I was over the top.

Annie And what about G and square-head. I suppose you think that's acceptable?

Rosie No need to get personal, Annie. Sure everyone in New York has affairs. When in Rome ... It's no big deal.

Annie But our Denise is Irish. So it's a big deal for her — or it should be, if she's got any pride.

Silence falls. They pour more drinks, adding mixing elements as before

Rosie Anyway. To go back to my problems. We'd press charges except we're scared they'd be released after the court case. We just pray they'll get into the charts and make enough to leave home. Meantime we stay out of their way as much as possible. Avoid confrontation — that's a tip I heard on the radio.

Annie Did you never chastise them when they were small?

Rosie I certainly did. They annoyed me so much one time that I broke a wooden spoon on one of them. A big, thick wooden spoon. I was devastated.

Dunya For Pete's sake — what's a wooden spoon cost? Fifty, sixty cents?

Rosie and Annie exchange looks

Rosie That's *hardly* the point. (*She pauses*) It was part of a set.

Annie And now they've turned on you. I'd say that's worse than Tony not talking or G having it off with your one ...

Dunya Hold on, girls. I think I've an emergency toke in my hand luggage.

Dunya exits

Annie (*drunkenly indiscreet*) I think she's had a facelift. Her eyebrows were never that far above her eyes. Did you notice? I thought there was something different about her the minute I set eyes on her.
Rosie Go 'way!
Annie Check it out when she gets back. Her forehead's too smooth for her age and she hasn't a sign of a dewlap on her jaw. A facelift, mark my words!
Rosie Can you imagine what a thing like that would cost a person!

Dunya's head emerges from the trapdoor. She enters, carrying another large joint. She presents her profile

Dunya Thousands and thousands of dollars and worth every cent.
Annie No! I don't believe it, you'd never guess!
Rosie Never! Have you had anything else done?
Dunya I had my ear lobes re-shaped. And veneers on my teeth.

The others inspect her head admiringly

And I had ... (*She sings to the tune of* Old Macdonald Had a Farm)
    A little lift here (*she cups her right breast*)
    A little lift here (*she cups her left breast*)
    Here a tuck (*she pats her right buttock*)
    There a tuck (*she pats her left buttock*)
    Everywhere a tuck-tuck (*she pats her stomach*)
Otherwise it's the same little Denise.
Rosie You know what I wish, sometimes? That we could go back to being close, the way we were when we were small.
Dunya The kind of sisters nobody would dare cross.
Annie I really used to look up to you, Rosie. When we were kids I thought the sun shone out of you, so I did. Now you hardly cross my mind.

Rosie And remember how Dunya used to make us laugh. She made up lovely little verses and parodies, from the minute she could speak.

Dunya (*as a lisping three-year-old*) Mary had a little lamb. It wandered down the shops. The butcher caught it by the tail. And turned it into chops.

Annie (*marvelling*) Composed at the age of three.

Annie mimes strumming a banjo. She sings a long "ohhhh" before suddenly breaking into the lyric, a parody of Jimmy Cracks Corn *country style*

> Jimmy cracks heads and he don't care.
> Jimmy cracks heads and he don't care.

The others stamp their feet to the beat

> Jimmy cracks heads and he don't —

Dunya
Rosie   (*together*) Care... His mammy's gone awah-eeee!
Annie

Dunya starts a new song, to the melody of Frère Jacques, *in which the others will join. First she struggles to find the right key*

Dunya Weee. We. We. We we we... (*She finds the key and sings sweetly and innocently*)
> We hate preachers, nuns and teachers
> They all stink, they all smell
> Always tryin' to spoil it, flush 'em down the toilet
> Down to hell. Down to hell.

Annie starts from the beginning after Dunya's first line, Rosie comes in after Annie's first line, and Dunya begins again after Rosie's first line, so that they are all singing charmingly, swaying from side to side

They trail off as they hear the church bells strike the hour and then the time, two o'clock

Annie places the tray containing the tea things, glasses, etc. on the floor, revealing a Ludo set on the table. She takes a dice and shaker from behind a leg of the table or the drawer

Dunya assists by putting the vodka bottle on the floor

Annie It's your turn to tell it, Dunya.
Dunya Are you sure it's not Rosie's?
Annie Positive. Rosie told it when we were here for Mammy's hysterectomy.
Rosie And Annie told it when we were here for Dad's prostate. So go on, Dunya.

All three close their eyes

Dunya (*dreamily*) It was an afternoon in August. I remember a shaft of sunlight shining down through the skylight. A shaft of sunlight with little motes of dust floating in it. I remember feeling soooo hot. Hot and bored.
Annie Mam and Dad were down the road, at Aunty Veronica's...
Rosie And we were up here, playing Ludo.

They now re-enact an incident from their childhood, playing themselves at nine, eleven and thirteen

They open their eyes and change position, their posture childlike as they lean over the table to play Ludo. Annie has first shake of the dice

The game proceeds for a few moments, then Dunya raps on the table. The three look towards the trapdoor, then at each other

Dunya (*airily*) Come in.

The Donahue Sisters

The three of them close their eyes to deliver the lines of their unexpected visitor, Dominic, a shy country boy, aged fifteen

The sisters create his presence on stage by speaking for him in unison, reacting to his movements, etc. Throughout the scene, whenever the sisters speak for him, unless they are moving, they close their eyes, the better to recall every nuance of his speech. It is clear that this is not the first time they have re-enacted the incident. As Dominic they are word-perfect and also recall his gestures

The stage directions hereafter will refer to Dominic as if he exists

Dominic enters and halts

Dominic (*softly, shyly*) Excuse me, but could you tell me where I'd find Mrs Donahue, please. I knocked down below, but got no answer.
Annie She's out. What do you want her for?
Dominic I've a letter for her, from my Da. He's the fella that fixed her chimney for her.
Dunya Oh, a tradesman with a bill, is it? Put it down there, so.

They giggle

Dunya indicates the downstage side of the table

Dominic moves towards it, Dunya ushering him with her hand

Rosie Are you hot?
Dominic I'm a bit hot, right enough.
Rosie Is that why you've no shoes on?

They giggle

I think the cat's got his tongue, girls. Would you like a drink of orange squash?

Dominic I would, please.

The girls produce three distinct gulps as of liquid being swallowed. They expel their breath with a loud "Ahhhh" and each wipes her mouth with her right hand

    Thanks very much. Well, I better be on my way.
Rosie Ah, don't. Stay here and talk to us.
Dunya Yeah. Stay here for a minute. Sure we're dying of boredom up here all by ourselves. What's your name?
Dominic Dominic O'Malley.
Annie I'm Annie and that's Rosie and that's Denise. The three of us are sisters. We've loads of talent. We dance and sing and everything. Do you know *Rum and Coca Cola*?
Dominic I've never had rum, but I prefer Tizer to Coca Cola.
Dunya (*mockingly*) He's never had rum, but he prefers Tizer to Coca Cola. We're talking about a song, you big dope.
Rosie We know every word of it. We sing it better than the Andrews Sisters. Put it on, Denise.

Dunya hops up and switches on an old Dansette-style record player. A record plays Rum and Coca Cola, *sung by the Andrews Sisters. Intro and Verse One. There's a distinct click each time the stylus hits a scratch on the record. Meantime, the Donahues arrange themselves in a line. They perform the carefully synchronised movements, reminiscent of girl singing acts of the Forties. They are really very good. They sing along*

Eventually Dunya swipes at the record player and it screeches to a halt

Dunya Well? What did you think? Didn't I tell you we were great? Everybody says we're a sensation.
Dominic Indeed ye are! Maybe ye could make a name for yourselves on the stage. Or even on the fillums. Put on three frocks the same and everything! Ye could be known as The Donahue Sisters!

The Donahue Sisters

Annie Have you got a sister, Dominic?
Dominic I have. Maeve, her name is. She's three. She calls me Dom.
Rosie Do you wish she was older … (*She ridicules his nickname*) Dom?
Dominic Sometimes.
Dunya Why would you like her to be older?
Dominic To be chatting with, in the house. To … play a game of Ludo with. (*He chuckles, pleased with his answer*)

The Donahues deliver a humourless echo of his chuckle

Annie If you had a big sister, would you give her a kiss?

They giggle

Dominic I don't know.
Rosie Would you like to kiss one of us, Dominic?

They giggle

Well, answer us. Would you like to?
Dominic I wouldn't mind.
Dunya Which of us would you like to kiss?
Dominic (*in an agony of embarrassment*) I don't know.
Rosie Guess who's the oldest of us three?

They react with smiles as if Dominic is looking at them, one after the other

Dominic Is it you, Rosalie?

They giggle

Rosie Rosie! I'm nearly thirteen. Denise is eleven and Annie's nine.
Annie Nine and a half.
Rosie What age are you?

 Me as Dominic

Dominic Fifteen.
Rosie Come on so if you want to kiss me.

Amid great giggles from her sisters, she stands and goes to Dominic

She arranges his arms around her waist and putting her arms around his neck, kisses him

The others make slurping, kissing noises

After a bit, Rosie staggers back breathlessly and resumes her seat

Was that nice, Dominic?
Dominic (*livening up a bit*) Yeah, it was. I bet you had jelly and custard after your dinner! I could taste jelly and custard!
Annie Now me!

She gets up and goes to Dominic and kisses him several times

Dunya jumps up and pulls Annie away

Dunya Don't be greedy, young one. Come on, Dominic, till I give you some experience.

Dunya kisses Dominic, then staggers away spluttering and wiping her mouth as if disgusted

They giggle

Dominic Well, thanks very much. I better be going now. (*He wipes his mouth with his right hand*)

Rosie leans over to Annie, whispers in her ear. Annie reacts with shocked excitement and passes on the whisper to Dunya. Dunya is acutely amused and can hardly speak

The Donahue Sisters

Dunya Will you show us your dangle before you go?

They giggle hysterically

Dominic (*indignantly drawing in his breath*) Indeed I will not!

The girls exchange looks

Annie You can't just come in here and kiss the three of us and then go. That'd be very bad manners. Are you from Railway Street, by any chance?
Dominic No.
Annie Well then, you shouldn't be having Railway Street manners.
Rosie I'd like to see his dangle.
Dunya So would I.

Dominic makes a move towards the trapdoor, but Dunya intercepts him, and shepherds him back

She pulls out the fourth chair, placing it DS *from the table, facing* US

Come and sit here, Dominic, in this nice comfy little chair.

Dominic moves to the chair and sits

Annie (*briskly*) Come on, then. Show it to us.

Pause

Rosie Will we count to ten, girls? One...
Dunya Two...
Annie Three...
Rosie (*quickly*) Four-five-seven-eight nine...
Dunya
Rosie } (*together*) Nine and a quarter, nine and a half, nine and
Anie three quarters...

They sit forward alertly

Dunya stands to see and backs away a little

Dunya Jeekers! Is that a big one or a small one?
Annie It's a big one.
Rosie I'd say it's medium.
Annie Sit down, you. Nobody said you could go.
Dominic I'll go if I want to.
Dunya You're not going till we say so. This is our house and as long as you're in our house, you'll do what we say.
Dominic I will not. I don't like any of ye. I'm going home.

Dunya dashes to the trapdoor and slams it shut

A snap lighting change makes the attic darker and more sinister

Dunya strolls back down stage, to Dominic's chair

Dunya I've heard that a kiss makes a fella's dangle grow. A girl at school says it's like operating a doorbell. You press one end and the bell rings at the other. Will we do it and see, Dominic?

Dunya slowly sits astride him and kisses him at length. The others crouch to get a better view

Rosie
Annie } (*together*) Jesus...

Dunya springs off Dominic's lap and slaps his face. Annie and Rosie create the slap with a clap of their hands

Dominic You're three brazen little rips. I'm telling what you made me do!
Dunya Will you listen to that fella? I'm telling what *you* did to *me*! My sisters will stand witness, won't you, girls?

The Donahue Sisters

Annie Course we will. Nobody'd believe a dirty little scut like you. Sure, boys are always doing dirty things to girls. Nobody would believe you, and you after coming in here with your bare feet.
Dominic Well, I'm telling on ye, and my mother will give out to your mother and she'll tell the nuns. Ye'll all get expelled. Ye'll all end up in a reform school.
Annie (*scared*) You bold boy! Shut up. Shut up. Shut up your big mouth!

She punctuates her speech with wild slaps at Dominic's body. The others provide the sounds by thumping at themselves

Dominic (*warding off blows*) Who do you think you're hitting? I'll say what I like.
Rosie If my sister tells you to shut your mouth, that's what you better do. We don't let strangers push us around. We've got our own motto!
Dunya
Rosie } (*together; chanting angrily*) All for one and one for all, the Donahue sisters stick together!
Annie

The three girls clap their hands twice, the outside two clap the middle girl's raised hands for the third clap. They stand US *of Dominic, linked like a fence*

Pause

Dominic (*softly*) I won't tell so. Let me go out and I won't tell.
Rosie How do we know you won't?
Dominic I'll give you my word of honour. I'll swear it on a prayer book.
Dunya I don't trust him. He's got skinny-looking eyes.
Rosie We can't let him out. He'll tell on us if we let him out.

Dominic moves and the three suddenly dash to stand on the trapdoor

They turn and slowly advance on Dominic as he retreats back down stage

Dominic (*pleading*) I won't tell on ye. Sure, why would I? I won't even say I was here. (*He gets angry*) Let go of me jumper before ye rip it ... stop it ... don't be pulling at me. (*He weeps*) I want to get out... (*He covers his mouth with his hand*) Oh janey, would you ever let me out?

The three continue to advance on him, with Rosie splitting off to approach from the left, a route that takes her past the doll's cradle

(*Softly*) Will I give ye sweets? Will I give ye Smarties? (*He panics*) Stop it! Stop it! Keep away from me! I'm warning ye, keep away from me now before I hurt one of ye!

Rosie arrives at the cradle and lifts out a big, porcelain-headed doll. She grasps its legs with both hands, as if arming herself with a club

(*Dunya and Annie only*) Leave me! Leave me! Oh Jesus, Mammy ——

Rosie swings the doll and smashes it down on the chair, overturning it. She freezes for a moment, when she sees what she has done, but then strikes the spot on the floor representing Dominic several times, with all her strength. The others stamp their feet, creating sound effects. Annie snatches the doll from Rosie and strikes further blows in an orgy of violence. The doll disintegrates, its red stuffing bursting out. Dunya grabs the doll and delivers more blows, jumping up and down with excitement. Finally they stand back, breathing raggedly. There is a long pause while they stare at their victim

Annie (*in a small voice*) He won't tell now, so he won't. (*She begins to suck her thumb babyishly, her forefinger stroking her nose*)

Rosie Mammy and Daddy will be coming home. What'll we do, girls?
Dunya We better hide him. Will we put him in a ditch?

Pause

Rosie We could put him on the road, under the bridge...
Annie (*excitedly*) And they'll all think a car hit him, the ejit!
Rosie We'll leave him up here till Mammy and Daddy are asleep. Then, when it's dark, we'll put him in the old pram under the stairs and wheel him down to the road. And we better put his letter back in his pocket.

The three move as if towards Dominic, with Annie sniffling sadly. They bend forward

Dunya
Rosie } (*together*) Awwwww... poor dolly.
Annie

Carefully stepping over Dominic's body, Rosie picks up the remains of the doll and crooning and rocking, makes her way to the cradle

The others follow, also stepping over Dominic. They help tuck the doll in, tenderly adjusting its bedding, patting it, etc.

Dunya
Rosie } (*together*) There now.
Annie

Using routes that detour around Dominic, the sisters resume their places at the table and sit back, drained and exhausted

The Lights come up

Dunya takes a handkerchief from her bag and dabs at her face

The three become adults as before

Annie collects the three glasses of vodka from the tray and passes them to the others

Annie As I remember it, I was the one who struck the first blow. Then Dunya.
Rosie (*firmly*) No. I hit him before you did, and Dunya was last.
Annie (*to Dunya*) I've always thought 'twas your go that finished him off.
Rosie You always say that when it's your go to tell it, but I think he was dead by the time Dunya had her turn.
Dunya (*yawning*) We have the same old argument every time we meet. What difference does it make?
Annie None, I suppose.

Pause

Dunya Show us what Tony does again, when he wants to know what's for dinner.

Annie performs three very rapid beef, chicken and fish mimes

Rosie The ejit. The stupid ejit.
Dunya And you say your kids are terrorizing you, Rosie?
Rosie Specially on Saturday nights, when they want money.
Dunya And then there's Guy. Dear Guy.

Dunya sits back, looking thoughtful. The others watch her intently

Annie Bold boys. All of them…
Rosie Very bold boys. I think we should put our heads together on this one, girls.
Dunya There'll be a bit of travelling. It'll be expensive, but that's no problem.
Rosie I'd like to travel, wouldn't you, Annie?
Annie (*enthusiastically*) 'Course I would. Sure, I've never been anywhere.

They smile at each other

Dunya
Rosie } *(together; softly and slowly, as children)* All for one and one for all, the Donahue sisters stick together.
Annie

They clap as before, one, two, three. But very slowly. Then suddenly they resume their Ludo game

Music, as used in opening, fades in

Rosie has first shake of the dice. She rattles it cheerfully and all of them are smiling gleefully as the Lights fade

They take their first bow seated formally as at the beginning of the play, acknowledging applause with a gracious inclination of the head. The second bow may be taken conventionally

CURTAIN

FURNITURE AND PROPERTY LIST

Further dressing may be added at the director's discretion

On stage: Child-sized table (with drawer). *On it*: tray with tea things and sugar tongs
Ludo board
Dice and shaker
Four little chairs decorated with nursery motif transfers
Doll's cradle containing soft-bodied doll with a large porcelain head
Other old-fashioned toys
Dunya's handbag. *In it*: cigar cylinder containing extremely large joint, lighter, handkerchief
Old Dansette-style record player
Old 78 RPM records

Off stage: Large bottle of vodka, three glasses (**Annie**)
Jug of tinned tomatoes, half a lemon (**Rosie**)
Large joint (**Dunya**)

Personal: **All**: wedding rings

LIGHTING PLOT

Property fittings required: nil
Interior. The same throughout

To open:	Black-out	
Cue 1	Irish children's choir *Bring up lights*	(Page 1)
Cue 2	**Dunya** slams trapdoor shut *Snap to low, sinister lighting*	(Page 22)
Cue 3	The sisters resume their places *Bring up general lighting*	(Page 25)
Cue 4	**Rosie** rattles the dice *Fade to black-out*	(Page 27)

EFFECTS PLOT

Cue 1	Before CURTAIN rises *Irish children's choir music*	(Page 1)
Cue 2	As Lights come up *Fade music; church bells in distance strike half-hour*	(Page 1)
Cue 3	**All** raise their glasses for a toast *Church bells strike quarter hour*	(Page 7)
Cue 4	**All** sing, swaying from side to side *Church bells strike the hour and then the time, two o'clock*	(Page 16)
Cue 5	**Dunya** switches on record player *Record plays* Rum and Coca Cola, *sung by the Andrews Sisters*	(Page 18)
Cue 6	**Dunya** swipes at record player *Music screeches to a halt*	(Page 18)
Cue 7	**All** suddenly resume their Ludo game *Fade in Irish children's choir music, as used in opening*	(Page 27)

MUSIC USE NOTE

Licensees are solely responsible for obtaining formal written permission from copyright owners to use copyrighted music in the performance of this play and are strongly cautioned to do so. If no such permission is obtained by the licensee, then the licensee must use only original music that the licensee owns and controls. Licensees are solely responsible and liable for all music clearances and shall indemnify the copyright owners of the play(s) and their licensing agent, Samuel French, against any costs, expenses, losses and liabilities arising from the use of music by licensees. Please contact the appropriate music licensing authority in your territory for the rights to any incidental music.

IMPORTANT BILLING AND CREDIT REQUIREMENTS

If you have obtained performance rights to this title, please refer to your licensing agreement for important billing and credit requirements.

CPSIA information can be obtained
at www.ICGtesting.com
Printed in the USA
BVHW040910220120
570183BV00014B/646